To: my sister

From: kaila

Happy Birthday!

I Love you!

May 19, 2010

Blessings
For Your
Birthday

Kyndall Rice

GIVEN TO

Birthday

OCCASION

May 10, 2010

DATE

Before I made you in your
mother's womb, I chose you.
Before you were born,
I set you apart for a special work...

Jeremiah 1:5

It happened before you were ever born. Before your
parents ever met. Even before the world had begun.
God knew you! He knew exactly what color your eyes
would be, how tall you'd grow—he even knew the
number of hairs you'd have on your head. And when
just the right time came, the master plan he held from
the beginning of time gave birth to an exceptionally
wonderful and unique person—you!!

To commemorate this special day, *Blessings
For Your Birthday* illustrates the individuali-
ty and wonder of every person in celebration through the precious pastel world
of Sam Butcher's famous characters.
Alongside inspirational scenes you'll
find encouraging words of Scripture
that capture not only the fun and
festivity of birthdays we share with
our earthly families, but also the
smiling face of our heavenly
Father who rejoices, too, in the
lives of all his children.

I sing
to the Lord
because he has
taken care
of me.

Psalm 13:6

May he
give you what
you want.
May all your
plans succeed.

Psalm 20:4

This is the day
that the Lord
has made.
Let us rejoice
and be glad
today!

Psalm 118:24

I praise you because
you made me in
an amazing and
wonderful way.
What you have
done is wonderful.
I know this very well.

Psalm 139:14

Every good action and every perfect gift is from God.

James 1:17

God wants everyone
to eat and drink
and be happy
in his work.
These are gifts
from God.

Ecclesiastes 3:13

Young people, enjoy yourselves while you are young. Be happy while you are young.

Ecclesiastes 11:9

Remember your Creator while you are young.

Ecclesiastes 12:1

I taught
you to remember
the words of Jesus.
He said, "It is more
blessed to give than
to receive."

Acts 20:35

But God gives us a free gift—life forever in Christ Jesus our Lord.

Romans 6:23

Thanks be to God for his gift that is too wonderful to explain.

2 Corinthians 9:15

Christ gave each one of us a special gift. Each one received what Christ wanted to give him.

Ephesians 4:7

God decided to give
us life through the
word of truth.
He wanted us to be
the most important
of all the things
he made.

James 1:18

This is what
God told us:
God has given us
eternal life, and this
life is in his Son.
Whoever has the
Son has life.

1 John 5:11-12

We rejoice in him.
We trust his
holy name.
Lord, show your love
to us as we put our
hope in you.

Psalm 33:21–22

Those who want
to do right more
than anything
else are happy.
God will fully
satisfy them.

Matthew 5:6

People who do what is right will have rich blessings.

Proverbs 10:6

You are
precious to me.
I give you honor,
and I love you.

Isaiah 43:4

Praise be to the
God and Father of
our Lord Jesus
Christ.
In Christ, God has
given us every
spiritual blessing
in heaven.

Ephesians 1:3

But you are blessed.
You understand
the things you see
with your eyes.
And you understand
the things you hear
with your ears.

Matthew 13:16

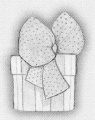

It is good to be
alive to enjoy the
light of day.
A person ought to
enjoy every day
of his life. This is
true no matter how
long he lives.

Ecclesiastes 11:7-8

The Lord your
God is with you.
The mighty One
will save you.
The Lord will be
happy with you.
You will rest
in his love.
He will sing and be
joyful about you.

Zephaniah 3:17

Don't be surprised when I tell you,
"You must all be born again." The wind blows
where it wants to go. You hear the wind blow.
But you don't know where the wind comes
from or where it is going. It is the same with
every person who is born from the Spirit.

John 3:7-8

They thought he had lost his mind. Jesus was telling the crowds that, in Christ, we actually can have—must have—a second birthday. Doesn't sound too bad, does it? But Jesus was speaking of a different kind of birthday—a spiritual one that happens in your heart when you give yourself over to him to cleanse and renew you.

As you give your heart to Jesus, an amazing thing happens. Your spirit is actually born again! What was dead before now has new life in Christ. You are filled with his Holy Spirit and with the desire to follow him with your whole heart. You are a new creation, and you now have two reasons to celebrate: one that you were born onto this earth, and the other that you have a new home reserved in heaven for you! So let the celebration begin!